Rabbit Turds

by Susan Froehlich & Jonathan Rodman

BEAVER'S POND PRESS

Rabbit Turds © copyright 2013 by Susan Froelich and Jonathan Rodman. All rights reserved. No part of this book may be reproduced in any form whatsoever, by photography or xerography or by any other means, by broadcast or transmission, by translation into any kind of language, nor by recording electronically or otherwise, without permission in writing from the author, except by a reviewer, who may quote brief passages in critical articles or reviews.

Edited by Hanna Kjeldbjerg

ISBN 13: 978-1-59298-557-9

Library of Congress Catalog Number: 2013908090

Printed in the United States of America

First Printing: 2013

17 16 15 14 13   5 4 3 2 1

Cover concept by Eric Dalseide and Jonathan Rodman
Illustrations by D.C. Ice
Book design by James Monroe Design LLC.

BEAVER'S POND PRESS

Beaver's Pond Press, Inc.
7108 Ohms Lane
Edina, MN 55439–2129
(952) 829-8818
www.BeaversPondPress.com

To order, visit www.BeaversPondBooks.com
or call (800) 901-3480. Reseller discounts available.

Dedication

I reflect on the joy that autism brings
How a son so clever can make my heart sing.
I think of the village who made him strong.
Jeannine and Bobbi were there all along.
Comforting friends in the challenging years
Saw me pull out my hair and hold back tears:
Victoria, Linda, Sally, Marlene
Janet, Pam, and, of course, Saint Jean.
Could we leave out Maggie, our lovable pup?
She inspires our poems and cheers us up.
My dear husband Dale is a stellar man.
He knows just when to hold our hands.
His faith in us, we took to heart
And now we've created this "work of art"
For mamas and papas, big kids and kiddies.
We hope you'll all love our silly ditties.

Contents

This Poem Will Save Your Life
By Jonathan Rodman 1

I Hate Veggies
By Jonathan Rodman 3

How Big is the Universe?
By Susan Froehlich 4

Dung Beetle
By Jonathan Rodman 6

Rabbit Turds
By Susan Froehlich 8

Pleading Eyes
By Susan Froehlich 9

There's Nothing to Do
By Susan Froehlich 10

Spence Toast
By Jonathan Rodman 12

Alice Blowfish
By Susan Froehlich 14

Operations
By Susan Froehlich 17

Smug Doug
By Jonathan Rodman 18

The Ghost
By Jonathan Rodman 20

Daddy Greenfingers
By Jonathan Rodman 23

Jennie G.
By Susan Froehlich 25

Would You Like a Half-Pound Burger?
By Jonathan Rodman 26

Hot Chick
By Susan Froehlich 27

Maggie the Pup
By Jonathan Rodman 28

Tommy Taunter
By Susan Froehlich 30

Zombies
By Jonathan Rodman 33

Grandma's Cast Iron Tub
By Susan Froehlich 34

Sharks
By Jonathan Rodman 36

Sundew
By Susan Froehlich 37

Japanese Red Bug
By Jonathan Rodman 38

Duck
By Susan Froehlich 39

Nattie Needleham
By Susan Froehlich 40

16 Boogers
By Jonathan Rodman 42

42 Toes
By Jonathan Rodman 43

Boobies
By Susan Froehlich 44

Crab Apple
By Jonathan Rodman 46

Security Breach
By Susan Froehlich 47

Crunch and Munch
By Jonathan Rodman and Susan Froehlich 51

Obsession
By Susan Froehlich 52

Sinosauropteryx
By Susan Froehlich 54

The Bumblebee
By Jonathan Rodman 57

Fantasy King
By Jonathan Rodman and Susan Froehlich 58

Down in the Dumps
By Susan Froehlich 60

Broccoli
By Susan Froehlich 61

Dawson's Bee
By Jonathan Rodman 62

Red-Eyed Green Tree Frog
By Jonathan Rodman 63

The Deadly Fly
By Jonathan Rodman 64

Marion the Vegetarian
By Susan Froehlich 66

Mindy Mock
By Susan Froehlich 67

The Peril of the Maiden
By Jonathan Rodman 69

Flatulence
By Susan Froehlich 70

The Angels of Crosby
By Jonathan Rodman 71

Zackie Zeek
By Susan Froehlich 73

Don't Worry
By Susan Froehlich 74

Pearl E. White
By Susan Froehlich 75

Thunderstruck
By Jonathan Rodman 76

Funny Bone
By Susan Froehlich 78

Sea Horse
By Jonathan Rodman 80

ZZZZZ...Ouch!
By Jonathan Rodman 82

Dog Paddle
By Jonathan Rodman 84

Woes of Scooping
By Jonathan Rodman 85

Silly Sal and Serious Sue
By Susan Froehlich 86

Shots
By Susan Froehlich 88

Dalia Smart
By Susan Froehlich 90

Maggie
By Jonathan Rodman 92

Frazzled Dad
By Susan Froehlich 93

Smeard the Beard
By Jonathan Rodman 96

Bunking
By Susan Froehlich 97

Caterpillar
By Jonathan Rodman 98

Torrey's Bad Day
By Susan Froehlich 99

The Jilted Photographer
By Jonathan Rodman 103

Firefly
By Susan Froehlich 105

A Jillion, Gazillion Monkeys
By Susan Froehlich 106

Choices
By Jonathan Rodman 108

Twitchy Crawly
By Jonathan Rodman 110

Who Am I?
By Susan Froehlich 112

Party Girl
By Susan Froehlich 114

Mess
By Susan Froehlich 115

The Bountiful Gift
By Susan Froehlich 116

Peaceful Planet
By Susan Froehlich 119

About the Authors 121

THIS POEM WILL SAVE YOUR LIFE

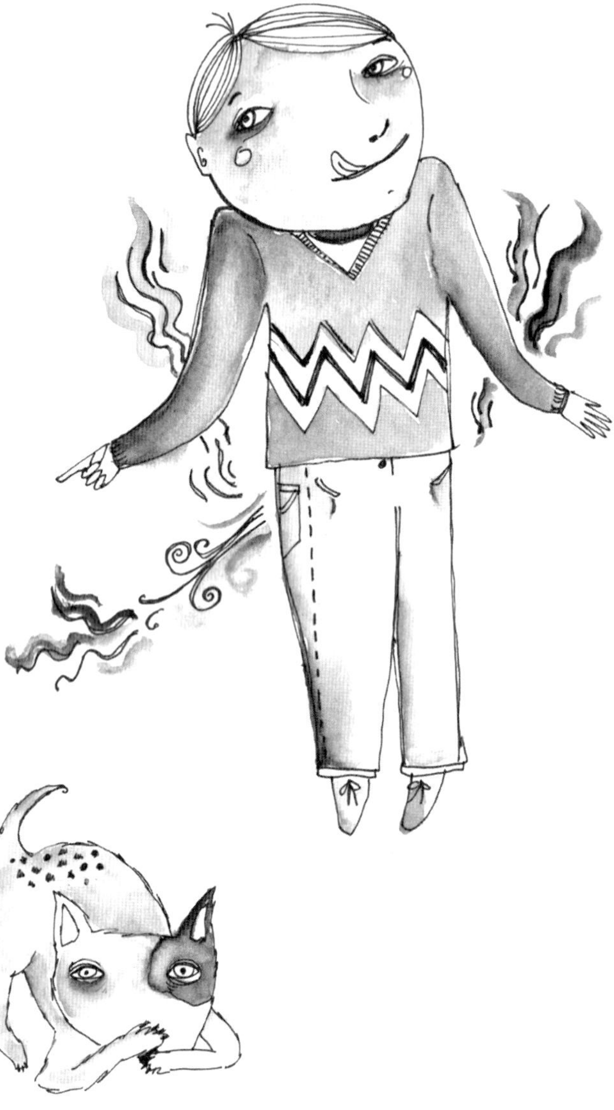

This Poem Will Save Your Life

By Jonathan Rodman

Timmy Sloot
Loved to toot.
When the toots were loud,
Timmy was proud.

His mother brayed,
"Stop tooting that way!"
So Tim fired off a custom excuse,
"Well, that one came from the dog's caboose!"

Timmy's mom frowned, and said, "Hold them in."
Though Timmy thought that was a cardinal sin.
For he had read
That excess gas should always be shed.

One day, Timmy's mom gave a harsh ultimatum—
It was so bad, I won't repeat it verbatim.
But let's just say, Timmy completely stopped.
For nearly a year, not a toot was dropped.

Then one day, Timmy had terrible gas.
"Mom, please, let me release it—it must pass!"

Mom said, "No, Timmy. Hold it some more.
Do what you're told, and don't unload it!"
Right after that, in a shower of gore,
You might not believe it, but
TIMMY EXPLODED!

Now Timmy's mom regrets the fate
Of her son who did not flatulate.
This wisdom she now sincerely imparts,
Is: "Always, ALWAYS let out a fart!"

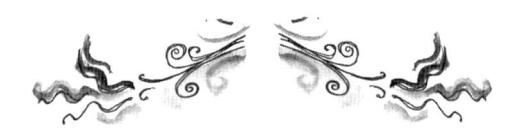

I Hate Veggies

By Jonathan Rodman

"I don't want to eat it."

"Oh Johnny, why not?"

"All I see are boogers and snot."

"Those peas are straight from the garden.
Eat them before your arteries harden."

"I wish veggies were sweet like fruit.
Eating green things makes me toot.
This is mushy.
These are gross.
Are you sure this isn't a lethal dose?"

"Eat them now or no dessert!"

"I suppose I'll try one...

How much can it hurt?"

How Big is the Universe?

By Susan Froehlich

HOW BIG
Is the universe?
I want to know.
Does it have a beginning?
Is it straight?
Does it bend?
Is it bigger than Mrs. Malkey's rear end?
How big is the universe?
Do scientists know?
Or do they just guess and put on a show?
Is it bigger than Texas or heaven or earth?
Was anyone there to witness its birth?
How big is the universe?
Does ANYONE know?

How BIG is the Universe?

Dung Beetle

By Jonathan Rodman

"Dung Beetle, Dung Beetle, agile and small,
How do you maneuver that massive brown ball?"

"Tenacity is in my DNA.
When it comes to effort,
I go all the way."

"I am curious. May I have a taste?"

"No, I cannot spare my bovine waste."
This ball of dung I must chauffeur."

"And where, pray tell, are you taking her?"

"I'm taking her home to woo a lady.
She'll be quite a catch
For this beetle named Brady."

"I can only think upon seeing this ball
That she'll have no interest in you at all."

> "You always seem to doubt the truth,
> But you don't know my Lady Ruth."

"Once Ruth is wooed and so enthralled,
What will become of that savory ball?"

> "A dung ball formed in such magnitude
> Is the perfect place to raise our brood."

"Seems an odd place to nurture your young,
While living off a ball of dung."

> "Dung families always dine on feces.
> You might say we're a peculiar species."

Rabbit Turds

By Susan Froehlich

Funny bunny eats,
Then excretes,
Two kinds of pellets—
Hard pellets for waste,
Soft pellets to taste.

Rabbits require pellet ingestion
To aid in digestion.
Say, I have a question.

Does a bunny ever think
That his breakfast fritters stink?
Does he say "Mmm! Delicious!
My, these pellets are nutritious!"?

A rabbit's diet, you must agree,
Is nauseating to you and me.
I'd rather devour peas or beets
Than to eat one morsel
Of a bunny's treat.

Pleading Eyes

By Susan Froehlich

Her bowl was filled with kibble.
She wouldn't take a nibble.
Maggie looked as if to say,
"What's the deal with lunch today?"

"You know that I like chicken soup
And ice cream, just a little scoop,
Pasta, salmon, and burgundy stew
But a bowl full of kibble simply won't do."

Maggie knows her pleading eyes are key
To get just what she wants from me.
And sure enough, I fill her dish
With chicken, eggs, and tuna fish.

Maggie's as clever as a dog can be.
Her pleading eyes are all I need
To become a cream puff who defers
To a little, white dog with curly fur.

There's Nothing to Do

By Susan Froehlich

"I'm bored! I'm bored! There's nothing to do!"
Mom said, "I feel so sorry for you.
Wash the dishes. Sweep the floor.
Clean your room. Paint the door.
And when you're through,
I'll give you more."

Now when I'm bored, I find something to do.
I have ideas, more than a few.
I ride my bike or text Cousin Ben.
I read a book right to the end.
And when I'm through,
I call my friend.

I won't tell Mom that there's nothing to do.
Mom has ideas, more than a few.
Mom makes sure bored kids are busy.
Her list's so long it makes me dizzy.

What would you prefer to do?
Listen to Mom say, "Do the dishes,"
Or make a choice
And follow YOUR wishes?

Spence Toast

By Jonathan Rodman

Let me tell you about my friend, Spence Toast.
Stuffed animals were what he loved the most.
Octopi, bears, apes, a sugar glider,
Pandas, sharks, lizards, and a fuzzy spider.

For the fuzz, he was a true lush,
But how could he sleep in a bed filled with plush?
Well let me tell you, his obsession turned bad,
And this poem tells a story quite sad.

For one morning Spence Toast did not awaken,
Mom called him for breakfast, again and again.
She flew to his room and opened the door,
Met by stuffed critters from ceiling to floor.

All she could see was a multi-hued mound—
When she called his name,
Spence gave no sound.

Digging and digging into plush so varied,
She found that Spence was completely buried.
And if you wonder how fared 'ol Spence Toast—
Well, to find that out, you'll have to ask his ghost.

Alice Blowfish

By Susan Froehlich

Alice Blowfish has halitosis!
Though it's awkward, I need to say
What's on my mind, I can't delay.

Sometimes when I get a whiff
Of her bad breath, I wonder if
She is aware…
Halitosis is NOT rare.

What she eats may cause a smell.
Perhaps she is not feeling well.
Poor hygiene's another reason
She may be in bad-breath season.

Please Alice, do not get depressed.
Instead, here's what I can suggest.
Explore the reasons for this state
Of halitosis, do not wait.

See your doctor.
Ask a nurse.
For stinky breath is not a curse.

Find the cause.
This is the key
To an effective remedy.

Before you know it, you'll be free
From your malodorous malady.

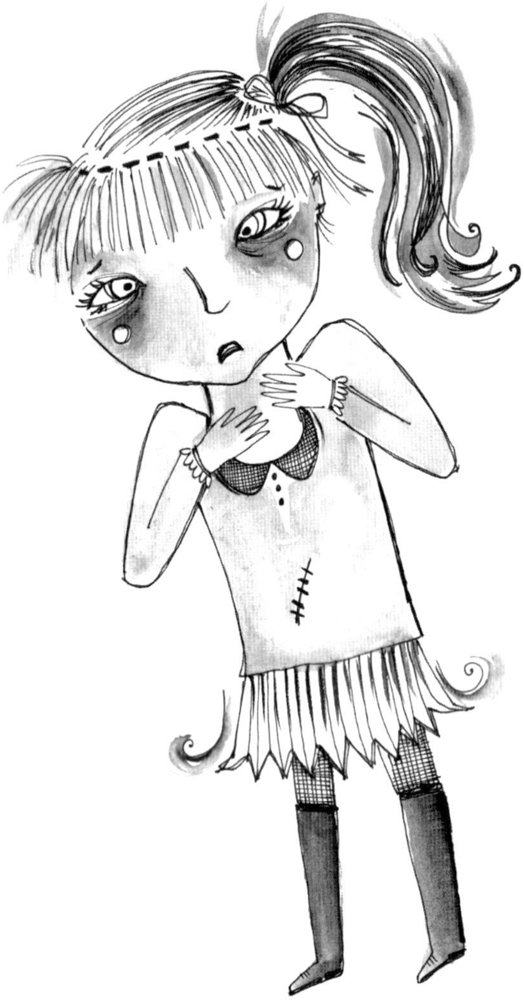

Operations

By Susan Froehlich

When my throat hurt,
I had a tonsillectomy.
When my side hurt,
I had an appendectomy.
When my head hurt,
I had a brainectomy.
Now my brain is in a jar
And I don't know where I are.

Smug Doug

By Jonathan Rodman

Last weekend we went hiking
With Pup Scouts, Troop Cedar.
Through the woods we stomped
Guided by our Pup Scout leader.

His name was Leader Doug.
The trails he did ignore.
He was pretty smug
As we tramped through the forest floor.

Into stinging nettles we went
And found our legs aflame.
We trudged up a sharp ascent
Greeted by thunderbolts and rain.

"Oh Doug, please let us go back!"
Doug replied in a voice quite shrill,
"Follow me, for I'm no hack!"
So we followed Smug Doug up a hill.

Bolts of lightning tore the skies,
Light and madness struck us blind,
But Doug ignored our chilling cries.
And left us in a terrible bind.

Though Smug Doug led our troop astray,
We managed to make it home that day.
A park ranger's skills and helpful aid
Saved our frightened Pup brigade.

Smug Doug's now a Pup Scout ghost.
Lightening turned him to human toast!
Here's some advice from my Pup Scouts and me:
There's a time to question authority.

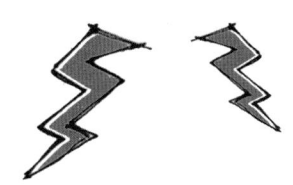

The Ghost

By Jonathan Rodman

Boo!
Who's there, is that you?
Just for a moment
I thought I could see
A wispy form
Pass straight through me.
It gave me a shake
And a terrible shudder.
All I could do was
Mutter and stutter.

Boo!
Who's there? What are you?
Why are you ha-ha-haunting me?
Do you have to be so creepy?

Boo!
Okay, that's enough of you!
I'm tired and want to go to bed.
I don't have time for things
Messing with my head.
So, please leave.
It's time for my reprieve…

All is silent now.
That ghost left quickly, and how!
Maybe I should not have been so rude…
But I was scared, and in a bad mood!

Now in this room,
I am the one and only…
And oh-so lonely!

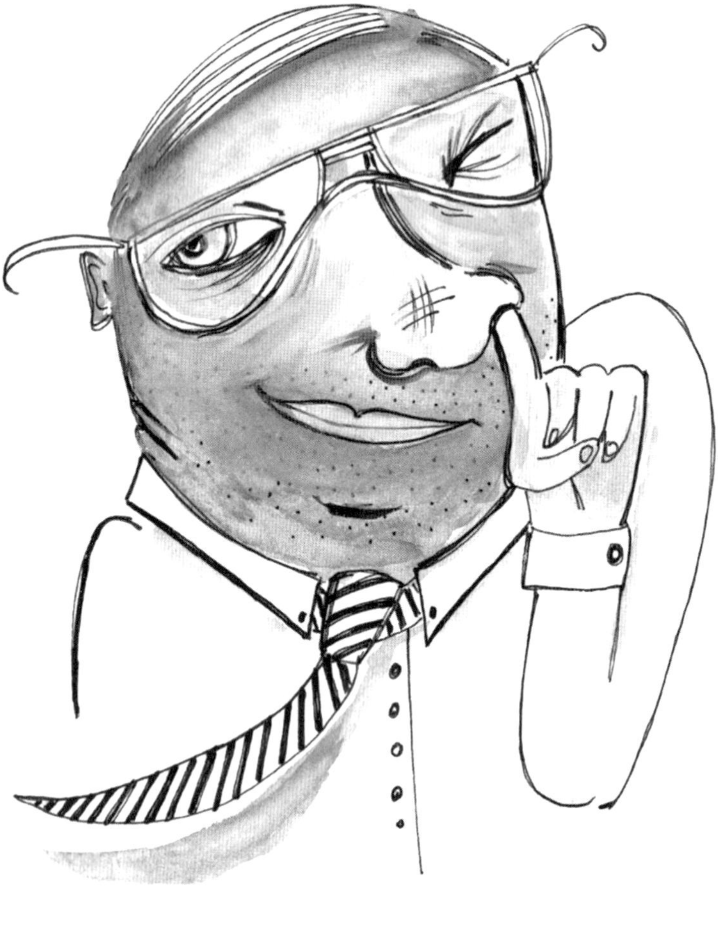

Daddy Greenfingers

By Jonathan Rodman

My dad is a man
With an obvious plan
To dig and dig and dig,
'Til his nose is red and big.

He thinks we don't see,
But his zeal is obviously
So great he can't refrain
From plucking again and again.

Round, big, green, and bright
Are the treasures that delight

My father the most.
But to us, it's just gross.

JENNIE G.

Jennie G.

By Susan Froehlich

Jennie G.
is
taller
than me.
She's
taller
than you.
She's
tall
as
a tree.
Oh,
I would
not wish
to be
Jennie G.

Would You Like a Half-Pound Burger?

By Jonathan Rodman

"Would you like a half-pound burger?"

I had a pet cow.
I named him Ted.
I loved him dearly,
And kept him well fed.
One day I came home
To see Ted in a truck.
I was filled with dread
As away the truck sped,
And my dad told me
What was to happen to Ted.

"I guess I'll have a salad, instead."

Hot Chick

By Susan Froehlich

How do you keep from laughing
When your sister thinks she's hot?
How do you keep from laughing
When the dress that she just bought
Makes her look like Big Bird
With its feathers tied in knots?
A yellow dress all poofy
With a satin bow so goofy.
Her butt looks mighty wide,
But putting that aside,
I've made up my mind
To try to be kind
As I snicker inside
While my sister gleams
In the dress of her dreams.

Maggie the Pup

By Jonathan Rodman

Maggie the pup,
With all your white fluff,
Do you think that you have
Slept quite long enough?

Your eyes bright,
With fur so alive,
Yet how little you move!
One might think you had
died.

When people abound
And food is around,
You hop and you run,
Your excitement astounds.

When guests go home
And the food is all gone
You return to a state
That fits a sad song.

The truth be told,
At the end of the day,
When lights are dim
And my mind is away,

I'd rather have YOU
Than a spirited pooch,
Eager to please
With a lick and a smooch.

If you ask me
If I would ever trade up
"No," I would say,
'Cause mine's the best pup!

Tommy Taunter

By Susan Froehlich

Tommy Taunter was very cruel—
The biggest bully in our school.
He put people down left and right.
Big and brawny, he loved a fight.
He picked on kids half his size.
He hurt their feelings and made them cry.

Why he was mean, I am not sure.
To say the least, he was immature.
He seemed to like to terrorize
Just so he could get a rise
Out of the victims that he taunted,
And he got just what he wanted.

One day, his classmates took a stand,
They refused to give in to Tommy's demands.
They made an anti-bullying pact
And this is how they resolved to act:

They found that silence was their best tool.
They didn't need to break a rule.
When Tommy was mean,
They appeared bored silly.
The room was warm,
But felt pretty chilly.

When Tommy made fun of Danny Stile,
They looked at Danny and gave him a smile.
"Come on, Dan. Let's go to class.
There's a test we need to pass."

After this happened a time or two,
Tommy Taunter didn't know what to do.
The thrill was gone
When the bystanders yawned.
He couldn't get a rise
From the kids half his size.
Tommy's bullying was no longer fun.
I guess you might say
The bystanders won.

ZOMBIES

Zombies

By Jonathan Rodman

Shambling along
Singing their sad song—
"Braaaaaaaains!"
They moan what they wish to claim.
Their smell attracts flies.
They don't care when birds
Peck out their eyes.
They will sniff you out
With their brain-sniffing snouts.
You can run, you can hide,
And many have tried.
Now they, too, walk slow
And zombie hordes
Continue to grow.

Grandma's Cast Iron Tub

By Susan Froehlich

Splishin', splashin',
Takin' a bath
In Grandma's
Cast iron tub.

Whishin', washin',
Soapin' and suds'in
In Grandma's
Cast iron tub.

Scrubbin', rubbin',
Rub-a-dub dubbin'
In Grandma's
Cast iron tub.

Quackin', yakkin',
Rubber ducks
In Grandma's
Cast iron tub.

Blowin', flowin',
Bubbles explodin'
In Grandma's
Cast iron tub.

Slippin', slidin',
Ridin' and glidin'
In Grandma's
Cast iron tub.

Singin', shoutin',
Clamorin' and clatterin'
In Grandma's
Cast iron tub.

Brother and me,
Careless and free,
Takin' a bath
In Grandma's
Cast iron tub.

Sharks

By Jonathan Rodman

Angel Shark is flat like a ray.
The Mako is fast and toothy.
The Nurse Shark sleeps throughout the day
While deep-sea Goblin looks goofy.

The Basking Shark is oh-so-big.
Bulls can be found in fresh water.
Hammerhead is a shark I dig.
The Blue Shark some like to slaughter.

None is notorious as
The powerful Great White,
But the Tiger is known
To cause quite a fright.

Most of these sharks I would not want to meet
Except for the Whale Shark,
Who doesn't have teeth.

Sundew

By Susan Froehlich

Flowering fireworks
Glisten in the sun.
An insect lights on tentacles,
A fatal error is done.
Delicious dewdrops
Bring bad luck
As the creature soon discovers
His legs are stuck.
From stuck to digested,
The prey is befooled,
Revitalized, the sundew
Shimmers like a jewel.

Japanese Red Bug

By Jonathan Rodman

To be a mom is a reward all its own,
Filling her nest with drupes like a drone.
Babies must eat,
Other moms compete,
But in the end, what's a mom to do?
Poor Mom is next on her baby's menu.

Duck

By Susan Froehlich

Daddy pulls up in his rusty truck
Pleased with his latest stroke of luck.
He shot a duck.
The feathers, he can't wait to pluck.
That means tonight we'll have to sup
On Daddy's duck.
Yuck!

Nattie Needleham

By Susan Froehlich

Nattie Needleham ate nothing for breakfast.
Nattie Needleham ate nothing at noon.
By dinner time, she changed her tune.
She was famished and couldn't eat too soon—
So she gulped up her soup and swallowed the spoon.

The spoon got stuck.
She couldn't breathe.
The doctor tried to make her sneeze.
Nattie Needleham sniffed peppers and chew.
Then it came: ACHOOO! ACHOOO!

The spoon shot out across the room
And hit the nurse with a bang and boom.
It knocked the nurse right off his butt,
And gave him a welt and an ugly cut.
Nattie Needleham said she was sorry,
But that's not the end of this silly story.

Nattie Needleham now eats breakfast and lunch
And in between finds something to munch.
She fills herself up with food that's yummy.
(Eating spoons is just for dummies.)
A spoon is not tasty.
A spoon can get stuck.

      And if someone shoots a spoon your way...
      DUCK!

16 Boogers

By Jonathan Rodman

16 boogers in a row,
16 boogers on my toe.
16 boogers in the sky,
16 boogers way up high.
What? You don't see them?
I know why.
I flicked 16 boogers
In your eye!

42 Toes

By Jonathan Rodman

My friend has 42 toes
And he's the only one
Who doesn't know!
Because of his nose
That grows and grows
Wide and large—
His nose is in charge!
He's going to the doctor
To get it reduced
To a size that is normal,
It can't be excused!
Life will be better then,
He supposed,
But then he will notice
His 42 toes.

Boobies

By Susan Froehlich

Two birds rocking back and forth
As they meet and greet:
They do the hokey-pokey,
Kicking bright blue feet.

Spy the blue-footed boobie
Looking for a mate.
He strives to make an impact—
Footwork wins the date.

The female gladly joins the dance,
Touching Boobie's bill;
A sure sign of acceptance,
The male bird is thrilled.

On the ground in a hollow,
Three small eggs are laid.
The parents take turns warming
Eggs throughout the day.

Parent boobies provide heat
By wrapping blue, webbed feet
Around their prized possessions—
Using feet for heat is sweet.

Six weeks later, eggs are hatched.
Chicks learn how to fish
Reaching into parent's throat
To snare a fishy dish.

Blue-footed boobies in the sky,
High above the sea,
Spotting schools of fish below—
Precise aim, you'll see.

And now the parents' job is done,
Boobies head offshore
To dive for small fish targets—
They're not babies anymore.

Crab Apple

By Jonathan Rodman

Crab apple, crab apple,
Sitting in the tree...

How is it
That you look
so yumm-ee?

Yet, when I take a bite
Out of your pretty green skin...
My puckered up face
Bares my chagrin.

Security Breach

By Susan Froehlich

We went on vacation, my family and me,
To a place far away, a shore by the sea.

To get there was easy,
No problems at all.
We flew on a big jet,
and we had a ball.

Going back home
was more of a plight,
'Cause the TSA
was in rare form that night.

Thousands of Agents Standing around
And just one little me with my feet on the ground.

I did everything right—
Or so I thought—
To no avail, 'cause of
something I'd bought.
I took off my shoes,
Put my bag on the belt,
I planned to sail through
What security dealt.

An agent in black
With a wart on his cheek
Waved me right through.
(He was kind of a geek.)

When I got to the belt
to pick up my stuff
I had a weird feeling
things could get rough.

My suitcase was stuck
in the security machine
With a fat, ornery agent scanning the screen.
His demeanor, first tiresome, turned out to be mean.

"Stop little man!" he said with a shout.
"Your bag looks suspicious. Now empty it out!"

"Put your arms up while I pat you down!
Pull your pockets out and turn around!"
I'll admit I was scared,
And starting to shake.
It was quite an ordeal
For a small boy named Jake.

Mommy and Daddy
Were having a fit.
They didn't understand,
Not one little bit.

"Little Jake's not a terrorist!" my daddy exclaimed.
"He's just a child trying to get on a plane."

The agent said sternly,
"Sit down, Old Man.
Your son is hiding contraband."

As all of this happened,
I observed quite a stir.
More agents, a dog and policeman came near.

They surrounded the bag with my stuff inside.
The dog sniffed and sniffed and then moved aside.

The agent in black
With the wart on his cheek
Gently opened the bag,
And took a small peek.
On top of the pile sat six pairs of undies,
Ten stinky socks, and some hotel sundries.

T-shirts and swim trunks were tucked underneath
And a pair of sandals
To put on my feet.

He picked up each item while wrinkling his nose
And filled a blue bin
With all of my clothes.

And that's when it hit me, how this fuss had begun,
At the bottom of my suitcase WAS MY BRAND-NEW SQUIRT GUN!

How the TSA scolded my parents and me!
They fined us for breaching Security.

I guess I was scared for a minute or two.
But now that it's over,
I have something to do.

A moral to share
From my trip gone awry—
Leave your squirt gun behind
When you plan to fly.

Crunch and Munch

By Jonathan Rodman and
Susan Froehlich

Two piranha named Crunch and Munch
Devoured goldfish by the bunch.
Regrettably, I did not heed
When Crunch and Munch were out of feed.
Now I have a solid hunch...
Crunch ate Munch for yesterday's lunch.

Obsession

By Susan Froehlich

Minnie Klindt collected lint.
No one could ignore
The stash in her drawer.
When the clothes dryer buzzed,
Minnie ran for the trap,
And emptied the lint basket
Onto her lap.
Caressing the lint,
She put it up to her nose.
Minnie preferred lint
To a freshly picked rose.
The softer the lint,
The better the feel.
Lint from a blanket
Made Minnie squeal.
She loved lint
Between her toes

And lint shaved from
Sweaters disposed.
But her favorite lint
Under the sun
Was the lint she found
In her belly button.

Sinosauropteryx

By Susan Froehlich

Imagine a dino with a lengthy tail
And a body covered with rings.
Imagine a creature who's not very tall—
A bird without any wings.

With tail feathers of orange
And a neck that's extended,
Lino the Sinosauropteryx's
life has ended.

He is no more.
He's out the door.
We've found his bones.
They've turned to stones.
And yet…

His skeleton's preserved,
And though we've heard
That a hundred million years have passed,
Lino's in our books at last.

Though he disappeared one day
His bones are surely here to stay.

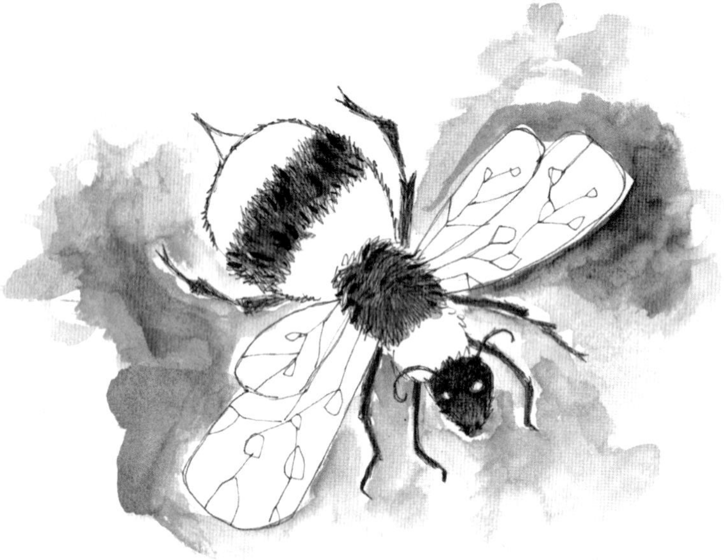

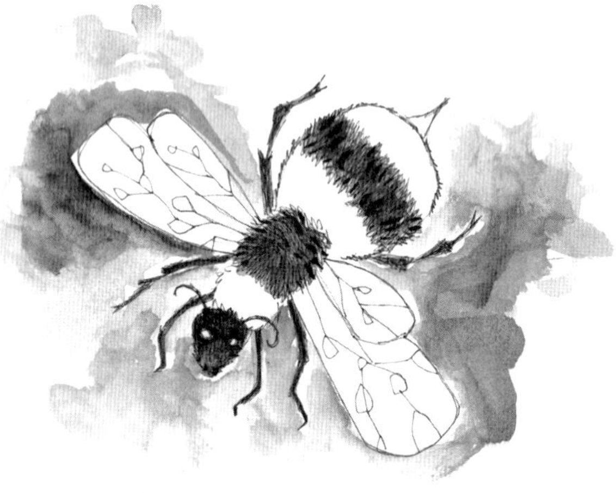

The Bumblebee

By Jonathan Rodman

Bumblebee, bumblebee
From where do you hail,
With your black stripes
And bright, yellow tail?

Fuzzy and round,
As cute as can be
I would like to pet you,
My Petting Bee.

Experience has shown
You could make me moan.
Your stinger would smart
And pierce like a dart.
You would hear my cries,
And now I surmise,
Better to pet a cold, hard stone
Than be shown
Petting a bumblebee isn't wise.

Fantasy King

By Jonathan Rodman and
Susan Froehlich

Barnaby Biscuits, a hardcore gamer,
Stayed in his room all day.
He didn't venture out to breathe in fresh air,
Indoors was where he played.

Hour upon hour, he carried on in the dark.
A monitor, the only source of light,
Brought perpetual electric sparks
And flashy monsters to fight.

With fingers quite nimble and skills so mad,
Ghouls, devils, and ninjas were prey
To Barnaby's high-tech game pad
As wars waged night and day.

Barnaby's friends worried something was wrong,
He'd been inside for years.
One day he stepped out, and it didn't take long
To confirm his friends' greatest fears.

The gamer's appearance sounded alarms.
No sleep and lack of sun,
Gave way to bowed legs and twisted arms
And pals who were utterly stunned.

"What is wrong with you, Barnaby Biscuits?"
A friend called out with a shout.
Barnaby Biscuits had contracted rickets
By waiting too long to come out.

Next time your screen says, "Continue?"
Be smart and don't hit "Start."
Get out of your chair and get some fresh air.
Just go to the friggin' park!

Down in the Dumps

By Susan Froehlich

Dismal, dreary, dark days…
One comes after another.
I wonder today,
With the sky so gray,
Why it's harder to smile
When the sun stays away.
I must take charge and not give in.
I've got to find a way to win.
I think I'll pretend I'm on the beach
With the sun beating down
On my head and feet.
I feel better already,
I've figured it out.
When the sun is away
I don't have to pout.
Dark days don't have to make me blue.
I don't have to be cranky,
I don't have to be rude.
Mind-over-matter is what I've found
To make myself happy when I'm feeling down.

Broccoli

By Susan Froehlich

If broccoli tasted like ice cream,
I'd eat it every day.
If broccoli tasted like ice cream,
I'd be healthy all the way.

If broccoli tasted like ice cream,
Vitamins A and B and C
Would live throughout my body
And take good care of me.

If broccoli tasted like ice cream,
I'd pig out 'til I threw up
And then a mighty green geyser
Would violently erupt.

That wouldn't be the end of broccoli,
But it would be the end of me.

Dawson's Bee

By Jonathan Rodman

Golden diggers in the sand
Await for a prize to emerge.
Out of a mound pops her head
And frenzied fellas surround her.
A riotous digger fight ensues—
Who gets the girl? Violence will choose.
In the end, after much bloodshed,
The gallant victor is stopped dead.
For where, oh where is his new lover's head?

Red-Eyed Green Tree Frog

By Jonathan Rodman

Red-eyed green tree frog,
Sitting on a branch.
Eyes of red, belly of blue,
Close yourself up
So danger can't harm you.
Around you swarm
A sea of pests,
Six-legged forms
For you to digest.
Open those eyes
And be real fast—
Eat up quick,
Or this meal
Could be your last.

The Deadly Fly

By Jonathan Rodman

What is a fly, do you think?
An insect that feeds on things that stink?
A tiny buzzer around your face?
A bug in your food as you say grace?

Some flies kill beetles with hard back wings.
Others kill bees, not minding their stings.
But the Robber Fly, known as Asildae,
Can kill much more than a bumblebee.

Beetles, moths, and damselflies decry
The deadly attack of the Robber Fly.
Grasshoppers, spiders, and butterflies, too,
Fear the Robber Fly through and through.

While in flight, engaging clear vision,
Robber stabs his victim with precision.
Into the helpless prey's body go juices
Turning innards into soup that splooshes.

The Robber Fly sucks up the soup as food.
Wouldn't you say he's terribly rude?

Marion the Vegetarian

By Susan Froehlich

Marion the vegetarian
Claimed veggies were the best.
"They're healthy for your body.
They're easy to digest."

Marion the vegetarian
Didn't practice what she preached.
By eating steak three times a day,
Her principles she breached.

I guess there was some conflict
'Tween her hunger and her head,
'Cause otherwise the food she ate
Would match the words she said.

Mindy Mock

By Susan Froehlich

Mindy Mock
Fell off the dock.
Kerplink! Kerplop!
Glub! Glub!
She sunk.

Lanny Lerout
Fished her out.
Swish! Whish!
Whew! Whew!
Mindy was blue.
Her cookies she threw.

And now Mindy Mock
is as good as new.

The Peril of the Maiden

The Peril of the Maiden

By Jonathan Rodman

Gunzo Kayden had a pet dragon
With a breath so foul, he burnt my wagon.
And even worse, he stole my fair maiden
And set her atop Mount Haven.
In a tavern where raised many a flagon,
A hero sat with his jaw a-braggin'.
Desperate for help, I asked his name.
He replied, "Sir Jaygon."
"Jaygon, please, my maiden's been taken
And she sits atop big Mount Haven
Awaiting the jaws of a terrible dragon."
Sir Jaygon just laughed and quaffed his flagon.
"Well thanks for nothing!"
My poor maiden was done-in
By the dragon of Gunzo Kayden.

The next time I want something done,
I'll do it myself.

Flatulence

By Susan Froehlich

Flatulence is a funny word.
Do you know what it means?
You may have heard.
Air in.
Air out.
Eat beans,
By all means.
Toot. Toot. Toot.
It's such a hoot.
And hence,
Excessive gas
Escapes your back.
Oops, alas…
When the odor's intense
And your friends take offense,
You'll know you've created
FLATULENCE!

The Angels of Crosby

By Jonathan Rodman

Three skaters,
Also the rink's creators,
Set to show the rest
Which skater is the best.

First is Dale who stands in place.
Then Sally falls flat on her face.
Susie's pride is tightly wound
As she skates around and around.

Next Susie does a fancy spin
Then glances where her friends had been.
A skater's smile turns to a frown...
Susie's alone on her proving ground.

Zackie Zeek

Zackie Zeek

By Susan Froehlich

Zackie Zeek
Is not a freak.
Although his demeanor is somewhat zany,
Zackie Zeek is extremely brainy.

Zackie Zeek
Is a gadget geek.
Hooked to gizmos from head to toe,
Zackie's a walking technology show.

Zackie Zeek
Has a wimpy physique,
An awkward stance,
And wears funny pants.

Zackie Zeek
Is a bona fide geek.
But by inventing gadgets the whole world seeks,
Zackie got rich in less than a week.

Wouldn't it be cool to be a geek?
Oh, how I admire Zackie Zeek!

Don't Worry

By Susan Froehlich

Don't worry!
Most dentists are quite polite.
They polish your teeth and make them white.

Don't worry!
A dentist is there for you
When your tooth aches and you cannot chew.

Don't worry!
A dentist will teach you to brush and floss.
She knows how to get her point across.

Don't worry!
If you want to keep your best-looking smile.
A trip to the dentist is well worthwhile.

Pearl E. White

By Susan Froehlich

Pearl E. White saw Dr. Fang—
The appointment started with a bang.
A six-foot needle jammed in her gum
Was supposed to make her mouth feel numb.

Then, with the aid of his cordless drill,
He made a hole the size of Brazil.
Then filled the tooth with casein glue
And told her to wait 'til she could chew.

When Pearl E. White's teeth got stuck,
She didn't give the dentist a chance to duck.
She punched Dr. Fang, and knocked him out cold.
She ran out of his office, and I have been told

That Pearl E. White never went back.
She reported that Dr. Fang was a quack.
He lost his license and went to jail.
And that is the end of this fearsome tale.

THUNDERSTRUCK

By Jonathan Rodman

Slumbering in bed, adrift, away...
  I waken with a start.
    My timid dog's begun to bark.
      I wait a bit. Does she want to play?
        From the bottom of the stairs,
          Trepidation is conveyed.
            Maggie Mae bounces, growls, and glares,
              No time now for hopes or prayers.
            I grab my bat for protection,
              And strategize intruder detection.

I steel myself to descend
　　The steps where I expect to fend
　　　　Against a thief, a murderer, or worse.
　　　　　I charge down to the living room,
　　　　　　Ready to face this unknown curse.
　　　　　　　Instead of certain impending doom
　　　　　　　　A bolt of thunder sounds KABOOM!
　　　　　　　　　My terrified companion barks again.
　　　　　　　　　　We're safe and I return to bed
　　　　　　　　　　　With my easily frightened canine friend.

Funny Bone

By Susan Froehlich

Joe's in a pickle.
His funny bone won't tickle.
When a funny bone goes kaput
It creates a problem so acute!
Joe requires urgent care
To live his life without despair.

Joe's in a pickle.
His funny bone is fickle.
If just a little smile he'd crack,
His sense of humor would come back.
Can I help? I'd like to know…
What would make you smile, Joe?

Would Daddy dressed as Fred Flintstone
Stroke your defunct funny bone?
Could a silly joke your brother told
Help your humor to unfold?
Would Grandma's ears tied in a bow
Prompt the smile you used to know?

I look at Joe.
He looks at me.
No hint of funny can I see.
There seems to be no remedy
For Joe's ill-fated malady.

The pickle jar is tightly screwed.
Joe's zest for life has been subdued.
Poor Joe is doomed.
He's filled with gloom.

Here comes a doctor who's acclaimed.
Joe's funny bone will be reclaimed!
The doctor inserts just in time
An artificial tickle slime.

Joe's not in a pickle.
His funny bone can tickle.
Ha-Ha, Tee-Hee
Ha-Ha, Tee-Hee
Joe's as happy as you and me.

Sea Horse

By Jonathan Rodman

I see a horse.
The horse I see
Is of the sea.
No, not a horsey,
Nor a horse sea,
But a sea horse...
Can you see?

A sea horse navigates its course,
Not with a hoof, but with a fin.
And when there's trouble it finds itself in
It changes the color of its skin.

And brace yourself, for if you find that odd,
You'll never believe the daddy's job.
Instead of Mommy giving birth
From out of father seahorse babies squirt!

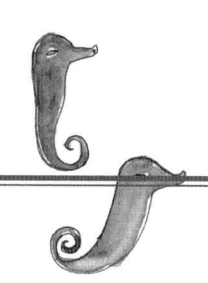

And not just one, you know,
Hundreds of babies from him flow.

So if you happen to be a guy like me,
And your day isn't going as you please,
Just be glad you're a human being
And not a horsey of the sea.

ZZZZZ...Ouch!

By Jonathan Rodman

Out of the sky you come
Diving death to some
But not to me, you see,
For I am the Stinging Bee.

What's that on my tail?
Just the throttle I nail.
When your hand of wrath follows behind,
Out of your reach I climb.

While you swat, and air is fanned,
I will finish my Immelman.
I drop down behind you this time,
And I vow to boggle your mind.

Then... you hear my buzz.
"Where did he come from?"

ZZ
   ZZZ
        ZZ
  ZZ
    ZZZ
         zzz
            zz
              z
                 zzz
                zzzzzz... ouch!

It's YOU I have stung.

Dog Paddle

By Jonathan Rodman

It's summer and the lake shimmers,
Beckoning me into its cool embrace.
I go, and though I'm not much of a swimmer,
I find solace from the heat in this watery place.

I float in the peaceful, liquid dark,
My mind at ease, my body feels light.
But then from afar I hear a bark
And from shore, I spy a shot of white.

Speeding my way, yapping wildly,
Into the water bounds a white fuzz ball.
She splashes yapping, paddling toward me,
My reverie is no longer serene at all.

But my rest is sacrificed to a greater end,
Because the lake is shared with my true friend.

Woes of Scooping

By Jonathan Rodman

I SCOOP
Ice cream and goop.
It hits my bowl and goes Ploop Ploop.

I SCOOP
My dog's smelly poop.
Stoop Swoop Whoop Scoop.

I SCOOP
Gook from a trench.
I am a troop
Entrenched in stench.

I SCOOP
A story for the news.
A crook has flown the coop.
I hope he's returned
Promptly to his group,
Lest he finds me out
For being a snoop,
And turns ME into a SCOOP of SOUP.

Silly Sal and Serious Sue

By Susan Froehlich

The most opposite sisters I ever knew
Were Silly Sal and Serious Sue.
Sally was wacky and made people laugh.
Susie was grave as a heart attack.

Sally told stories and acted them out—
It didn't matter what the tale was about.
She entertained friends who howled and roared
'Til their sides hurt and they could take it no more.

Susie was quiet, calm, and aloof.
She worried about manners and how her hair poofed.
Susie wore black pants and could not tell a joke.
She wouldn't bend the rules, not even when coaxed.

Sally and Susie had some things they shared,
Though they were different when they were compared.
Both measured the same on the chart by the door
And they loved to turn cartwheels on Mom's polished floor.

They both loved their families as much as they could,
And they loved each other as two sisters would.
You see, opposite sisters can be best friends, too.
Just ask Silly Sal and Serious Sue.

SHOTS

By Susan Froehlich

From the day I remember the first one I got,
I hate, I hate, I HATE getting shots.
To tell the truth, the pain's not so bad—
A stick with a needle stings just a tad.
It's the very idea that gives me the shivers,
My hands are trembling while my chin quivers.

I wait in line and roll up my sleeve
I may look away, but I always see
That needle aiming directly at me.
And so, like always, I tense up and moan.
Mom says I'll get over it once I am grown.

The alternative, of course, is to get very sick
I'd like to see heaven, but not lickety split.

So I'll put on a brave face and stick out my arm
As long as I know it will keep me from harm.

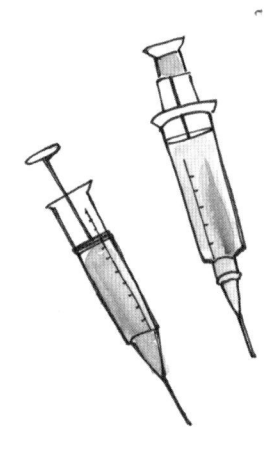

Dalia Smart

By Susan Froehlich

Dalia Smart reads twelve books a day.
With her nose in a book, she goes out to play.
Dalia reads while she swings.
She reads while she sings.
She reads in the shower
For more than an hour.
She reads in the dark by the light of the moon.
She reads every moment from July to June.

Dalia Smart's backpack is filled to the brim
With eleven books bundled tightly within.
The twelfth book rests in the palm of her hands
While she's reading of faraway places and lands.
Her passion for books is not overblown.
Indeed, Dalia lives in the Reading Zone.

Dalia Smart has a good last name
But a name won't give you a claim to fame.
Dalia's smart 'cause she avidly reads
Books with titles from A to Z.
Dalia holds a key to succeed—
It's all in the books she chooses to read.
You can be smart like Dalia, too.
Just pick up a book and read it through.

Maggie

By Jonathan Rodman

Fuzzle Muzzle,
Dribbly Guzzle.
Bark and Yip,
Sip and Skip.
Doggie Do and
Doggie Don't.
Whirlwind Coaster,
Silly Boaster,
Crying, Sighing,
Yapping, Crapping,
Cuddly, Bubbly,
Maggie's My Buddy.

Frazzled Dad

By Susan Froehlich

"It's time for bed," my daddy said.
I crawled on the bunk and under the spread.
"Read me a story," I said. "Pretty Pleazzzze!"
Dad read me a story about bumble bees.

"Now go to sleep. The day is done.
Good night, Harry. Sleep tight, Son."
When Dad took off down the hall,
I was not sleepy— not weary at all.

BAAaaaaaa

I jumped up and down 'til I hit my head.
I hit it so hard that my thick head bled.
I began to holler and blubber and wail.
Dad tried to calm me, to no avail.

"Now settle down, Son, and go to sleep.
Close your eyes and start counting sheep."
I closed my eyes and counted to ten.
I counted sheep time and again.

The sheep were making quite a commotion
Expressing all their silly emotions
BAAaaaa BAAaaaaa, here and there.
They were so loud, they hurt my ears.

What could I do to stop the noise?
I got out of my bed and played with my toys.
The toys kept me busy for an hour or two.
By then I was weary through and through.

I returned to my bed and snuggled on in.
But my mind wasn't quiet; it started to spin.
I thought about this and I thought about that.
Inside my head, I heard CHAT CHAT CHAT.

Dad came by on his way to his room.
When he saw I was up, he started to fume.
Dad wanted to see his kid asleep.
He didn't want me to make a peep.

But how's a kid supposed to sleep
With a bed that's bouncy and bleating sheep
And a floor covered with toys two feet deep?

Bedtime is more for dad than me.
Dad needs peace and time to be free.
Dad wants me to fall fast asleep.
But sleeping's a promise I cannot keep.

Smeard the Beard

By Jonathan Rodman

Smeard's striking red beard stood out in a crowd.
It was fluffy and full and made him proud.
Smeard himself was a stout young dwarf.
His clan hailed from the mountains of Gworf.
They were the great Metre Kind
And in their annals, you would find
Records of them besting other clans
In every game throughout the land.
They threw axes the furthest
And ate the most in the great Gut Burstest
Little Smeard was the pride of his clan
No dwarf could grow a beard so grand.
This one special trait earned him glory.
His beard stayed long even when it grew hoary.
If you sometime feel you aren't that great
And that mediocrity is your fate
Find just one thing that creates a buzz
Like Smeard the Beard and his bushy chin fuzz.

Bunking

By Susan Froehlich

I'm
safe
in the
top bunk,
way up high,
above my brother,
close to the sky.
No need
to fear
critters
under my bed,
'cause little brother
is down there instead.
Oh, dear,
Now I fear...
What if...
the giraffes and
the butterflies
find me here?

Caterpillar

By Jonathan Rodman

Cater
Catter pillar patter
From whence have you come, legs a smatter?
An inkling I have to make you splatter.
But then such a slight
Maybe just might
Hinder you
Before you take flight.
Oh, beautiful butterfly...
What a sight!

Torrey's Bad Day

By Susan Froehlich

Torrey awakened ten minutes late.
He had to get ready by half past eight.
Dirty clothes piled on the floor in a mound,
With the least dirty underwear yet to be found.

To make matters worse,
The cat took a squirt,
Right on, you guessed it,
His favorite T-shirt.

Oh my, what's the topping on Torrey's Pop-Tart®?
A mouse must have gotten a little head start.
In a brown paper bag, Torrey packed his lunch—
A sandwich, a pear, and a box of fruit punch.

In his rush, Torrey left the freshly-packed sack
On the desk right next to his brand new Mac.
He ran to the bus stop at 8:26
And the neighborhood bully was waiting with tricks.

Luckily, the bus arrived right away.
At least one thing went right
On that miserable day.

Torrey got to class and opened his pack.
Reading was something he knew he could hack.
He took out his book and followed along.
The teacher asked a question,
Torrey answered it wrong.

He spent the lunch hour begging for food.
Some kids were kind,
While others were cruel.
He asked Blake Patrick for a bite of his cake.
Blake promptly replied,
"Go jump in the lake."

Gym class followed lunch that day.
Torrey was the last one chosen
For the running relay.
Torrey tried hard to run very fast.
In spite of his effort, his team came in last.

In math class
He took a challenging test.
He was sure of ONE answer
And guessed at the rest.

The last period was band.
Torrey banged on the drum.
When the band started playing,
He did something dumb.
He hit the drum with too much force.
It punctured a hole in the drum, of course.

When the school bell rang
Torrey sighed with relief.
However, his reprieve
Was remarkably brief.

He sorted through homework
And packed up his stuff.
When he ran outside,
He had missed the bus.

Torrey walked thirty-two blocks to his home
To find his family had moved to Rome.
After all this,
I guess you could say...

A kid named Torrey had a very bad day.

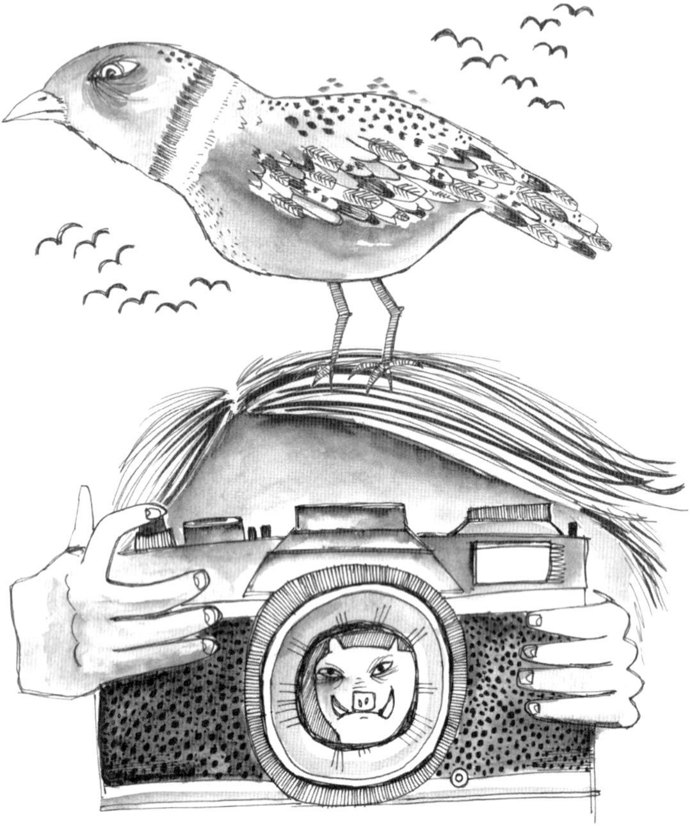

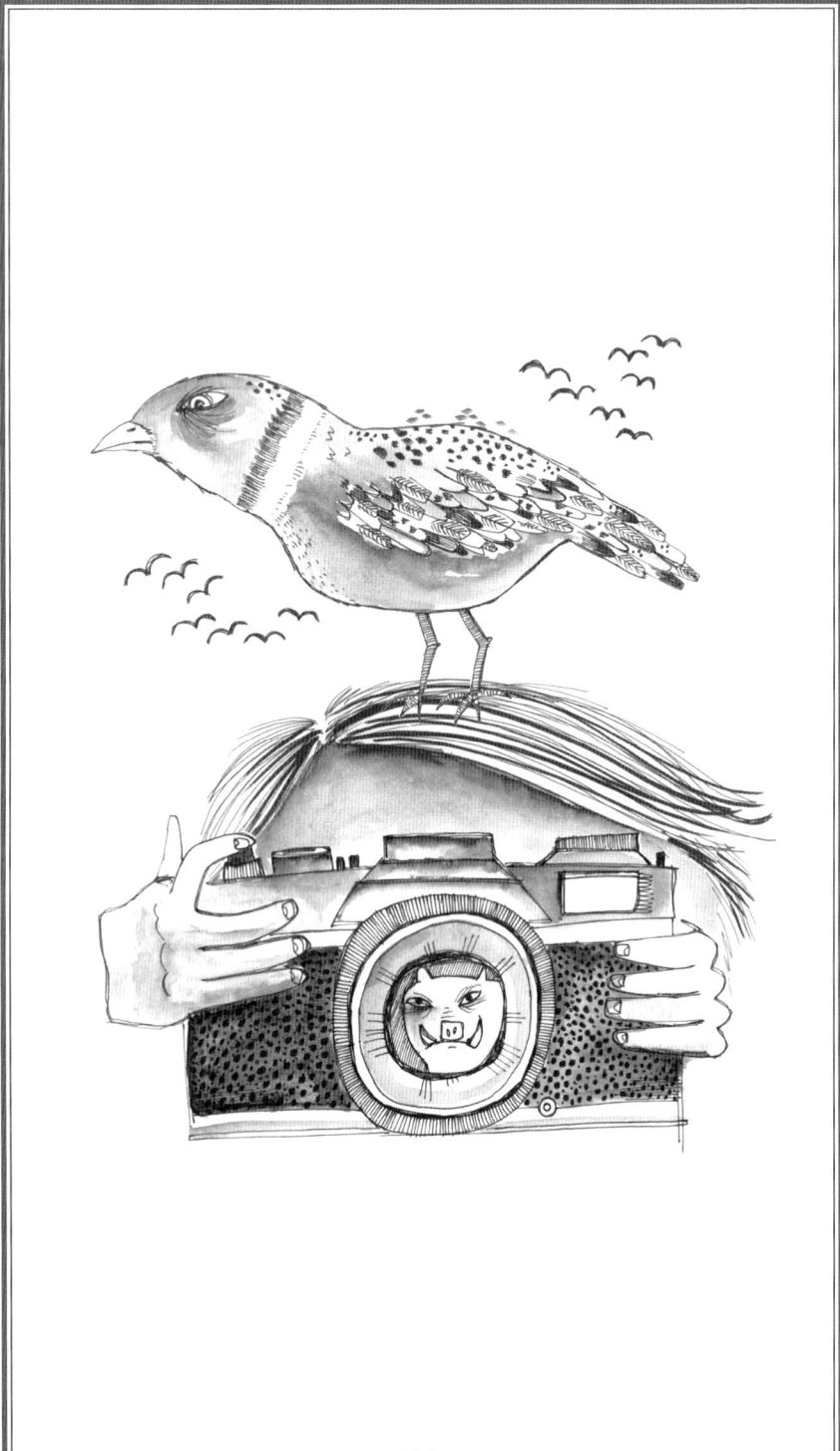

The Jilted Photographer

By Jonathan Rodman

They say a picture's worth a thousand words,
But what about a picture of two thousand birds?
And could a picture of a million boar
Be worth even more?

Next time I take a picture of a thousand bees,
Appraise it at a million words, if you please.
Even then, you know how I'd feel?
I'd say, "Hey, I got a bad deal."

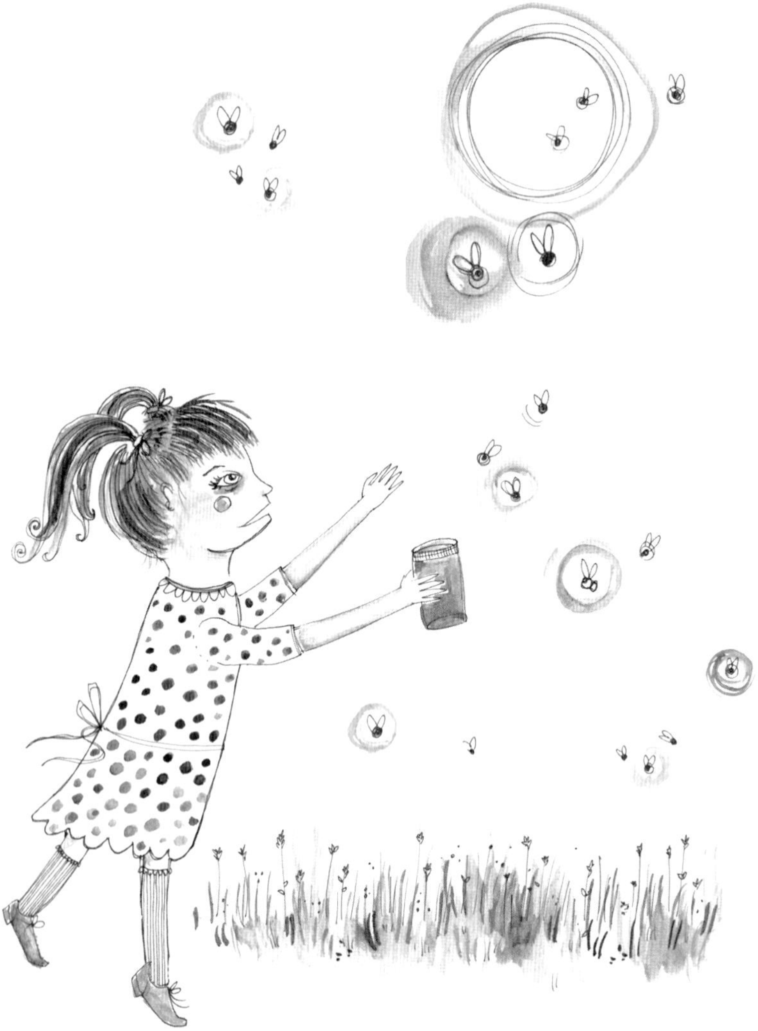

Firefly

By Susan Froehlich

Firefly, firefly,
Flaunting flashing lights.
It's fun to chase you in the grass
On warm and balmy nights.

Firefly, firefly,
Let me catch you, please.
I'll put you in a bug jar
Where you can breathe with ease.

Firefly, firefly,
I'll watch you from my bed.
Your glow will keep me warm,
But in the morning you'll be dead.

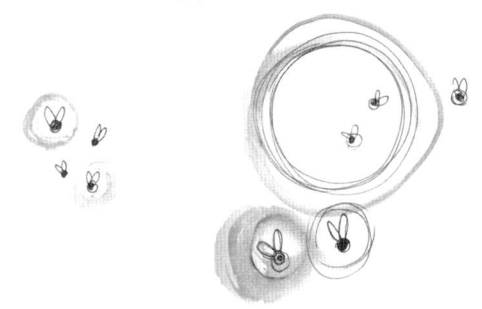

A Jillion, Gazillion Monkeys

By Susan Froehlich

A jillion, gazillion monkeys
Hanging from the trees,
Filling up our breathing space,
Doing what they please.

Monkeys perched on each rooftop.
Monkeys drinking soda pop.
A million monkeys on display
A thousand, thousand here to stay.

A million monkeys in the trees,
Creating babies, one, two, three.
My brain fails to comprehend
A billion monkeys end-to-end.

A trillion monkeys seems insane,
More than our planet could sustain.
A trillion monkeys multiply—
Now a quadrillion exist worldwide.

This problem could go on and on,
New monkeys born from dusk 'til dawn.
So many monkeys, limited space,
No more room for the human race.

This great world, once our domain,
Now is where the monkeys reign.
To planet Earth, we bid adieu,
A new abode we must pursue.

It won't be long and we'll embrace
A distant home in outer space.

Choices

By Jonathan Rodman

Let's go the movies.
What should we see?
I like to laugh, so maybe a comedy.
You like watching things blow up,
But some movies are gross and make me throw up.
Then there's horror, but that's so scary…
Just no romantic comedies,
We'll be forced into those after we marry.
I wish we could see one that's obscene,

But we have to wait until we're eighteen.
We could see a war epic, but that might get long.
And no musicals, 'cause I hate movies with songs.
I want to see one with action and laughs,
Or a film about wildlife, cats, or giraffes.
I wouldn't mind a sentimental sigh
How about a cartoon, but no CGI.
CGI is just visual chotsky,
The best anime films are made by Miyazaki.
We could check the star ratings or read the reviews
And use recommendations to help us choose.
Hey, do you have money to pay for the show?
Neither do I, I guess we can't go!

Twitchy Crawly

By Jonathan Rodman

Do you have a tic?
It makes you nervous,
And may make me sick.
So do me a service
And stop that tic, right quick.
What do you mean you can't?
Perhaps with a candlestick...

Oh,
    there's
    another
    one
    crawling
    up
    your
    pants...
    t
    i
    c
    k

Who Am I?

By Susan Froehlich

I'm a powerful predator
Who lives in the sea.
All kinds of creatures
Are fearful of me.

Weighing six tons,
I'm enormous, all right.
I could fit in a bus,
Though it'd be tight.

Black and white
With a dorsal fin,
I hunt with friends,
I hunt with kin.

Birds and fish
Are what I eat.
Marine mammals
Are my favorite treat.

I talk to my friends
Through special tones,
Whistle and click,
Grunt and moan.

I relish my freedom
to swim all day,
So please don't put me
On display.

With all these clues
in ample detail,
Who am I?

                          I'm Orca, a killer whale! (upside down)

Party Girl

By Susan Froehlich

Party Girl eagerly waits at the door
For guests to arrive at half past four.
When the first group arrives, her role is clear—
Making sure callers feel welcomed with cheer.

Bouncing her greeting with a yip and a yap,
Maggie makes rounds from lap to lap,
Quickly becoming the belle of the ball,
Commanding attention from one and all.

Party Girl can't seem to settle down,
Splattering wine on a lady's fine gown.
Mom spots the dog harassing the guests,
So Maggie is clothed in her holiday dress.

The life of the party's not dancing around,
In excitement's place is a doggy frown.
"In this silly dress, I'm completely bummed out—
For the rest of the evening, I'll sit here and pout."

Mess

By Susan Froehlich

"You need to declutter!" my mommy declares.
"Go straight to your room and start with your bears!
Have you played with them lately?
That is the test.
Store in these boxes when the answer is yes.
When the answer is no, the bears have to go.
Then move to your games and movies and toys.
Sort and straighten them,
Pile them up high.
You'll feel so good when it's all organized."
I'm surrounded by stuff and heave a big sigh.
My mom says, "Declutter!" and I want to cry.
I love all my stuff and won't give it away.
So I stay in my room and play all day.

The Bountiful Gift

By Susan Froehlich

A chunky gerbil in a cage
Was my all-time favorite gift.
Mommy couldn't force a smile,
I'm sure you catch my drift.

I named my gerbil Bridget.
I tried to meet her needs.
I filled one bowl with water
And another one with seeds.

I put her in my pocket
And took her for a stroll.
At night, I locked her in her cage
And prayed for her gerbil soul.

The next morning I arose
To an awfully big surprise.
The cage was overflowing
With baby gerbil gals and guys.

Not one, not two, not four, nor five
Baby gerbils did I see.
Nine baby gerbils had been born—
A special gift for me.

Mom spotted my presents
And was totally outraged.
Somehow she couldn't accept
Nine pups of newborn age.

Now I need to find a home
For every gerbil born.
Would you like a gerbil for free?
But don't tell your mom 'til the morn.

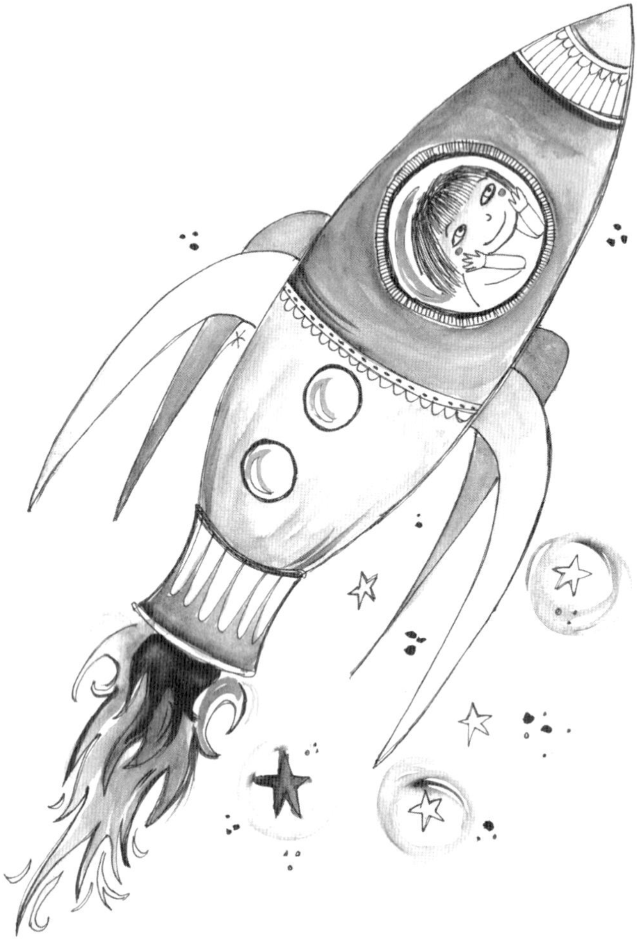

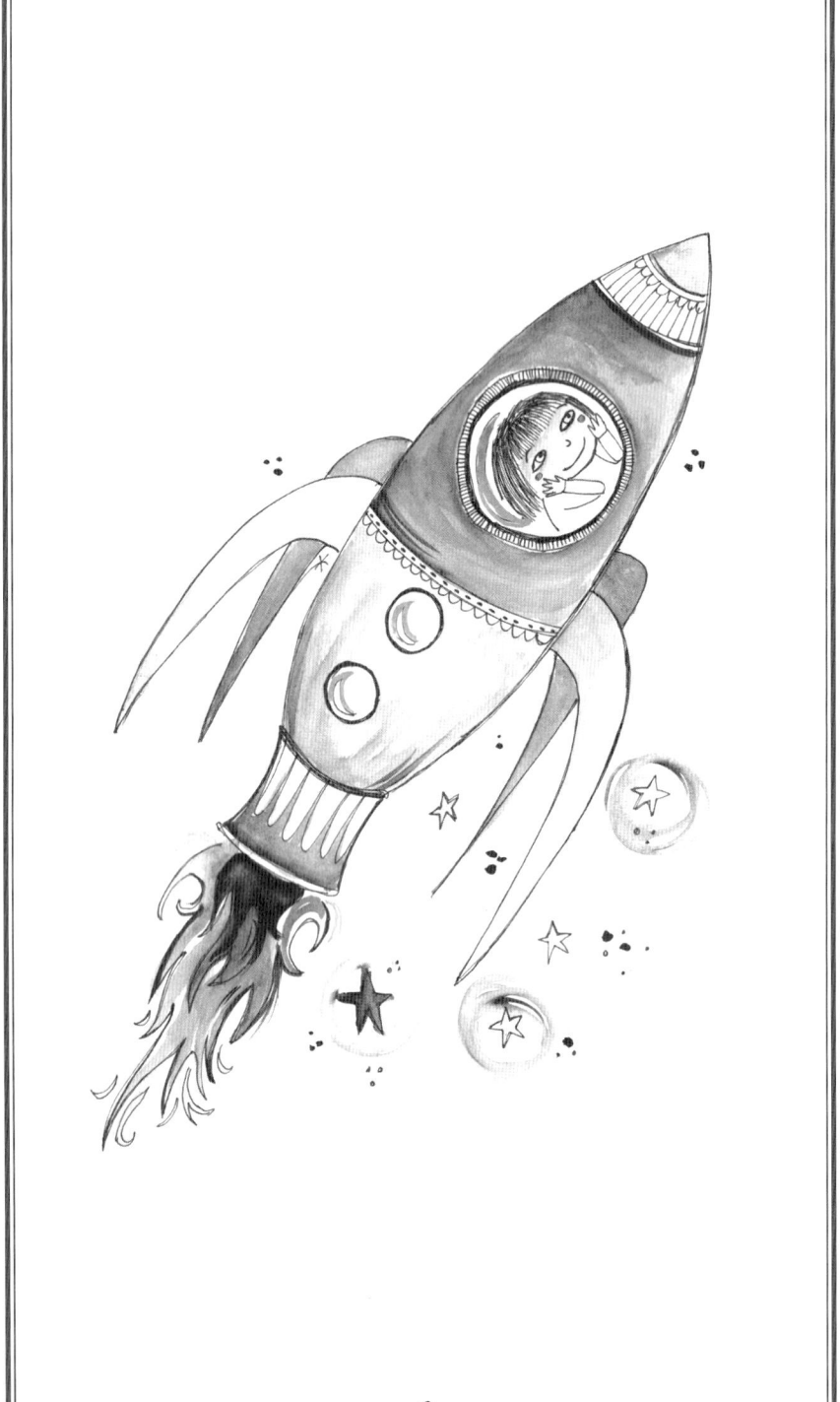

Peaceful Planet

By Susan Froehlich

Over the moon and under the stars,
This rocket will take me to planet Mars.
To get there will take nearly three hundred days,
But when I arrive, I plan to stay.
Planet Mars is a peaceful place
No wars, no crime, no bullies to face.
On Mars, I'll be completely free,
Just the sun and the stars and little ol' me.

About the Authors

Rabbit Turds was written by Susan Froehlich and her autistic son Jonathan Rodman. When her children were young, Susan read to Jon and his two younger siblings from Shel Silverstein's *Where the Sidewalk Ends* until the pages were worn and tattered. Jonathan's early love of literature developed into an exceptional talent for writing, and today Susan and Jonathan spend hours together researching topics and writing poems. They hope that people will enjoy reading this book as much as they enjoyed creating it.

Susan has worked with children with learning talents and challenges as the co-owner and Executive Director of Sylvan Learning Center.

Rabbit.Turds@Yahoo.com